MY NOISY BODY

LIZA FROMER AND FRANCINE GERSTEIN MD
Illustrated by Joe Weissmann

TUNDRA BOOKS

Published in Canada by Tundra Books,
75 Sherbourne Street, Toronto, Ontario M5A 2P9

Published in the United States by Tundra Books of Northern New York,
P.O. Box 1030, Plattsburgh, New York 12901

Library of Congress Control Number: 2010940341

Library and Archives Canada Cataloguing in Publication

Fromer, Liza
        My noisy body / Liza Fromer and Francine Gerstein ; illustrated by
Joe Weissmann.

(Body works)
ISBN 978-1-77049-201-1   4766 9972 ¹/₁₂

        1. Human body – Juvenile literature. 2. Human physiology – Juvenile
literature. 3. Human anatomy – Juvenile literature.
I. Gerstein, Francine II. Weissmann, Joe, 1947- III. Title.
IV. Series: Body works (Toronto, Ont.)

QP37.F766 2011   j612   C2010-907306-1

We acknowledge the financial support of the Government of Canada through the Book
Publishing Industry Development Program (BPIDP) and that of the Government of Ontario
through the Ontario Media Development Corporation's Ontario Book Initiative.
We further acknowledge the support of the Canada Council for the Arts and the Ontario
Arts Council for our publishing program.

ONTARIO ARTS COUNCIL
CONSEIL DES ARTS DE L'ONTARIO

Medium: watercolor on paper

Design: Leah Springate

Printed and bound in China

1 2 3 4 5 6   16 15 14 13 12 11

Also available in this Body Works series by Liza Fromer
and Francine Gerstein MD, illustrated by Joe Weissmann

Authors' Note

The information in this book is to help you understand your body and learn why it works the way it does.

It's important that you see your family doctor at least once each year. If you're worried about your health or think you might be sick, speak to an adult and see your doctor.

Have you ever wondered why your body makes so many weird noises? Burps, hiccups, stomach growls, and farts – with all that noise, it's a wonder you ever get any sleep! You know that your voice can make lots of wonderful noises, but so can the rest of your body.

When your body makes noise, it's doing what comes naturally – and sometimes that can be loud. It's nothing to be embarrassed about because everyone's body does the same jobs! So when your body gets noisy, just say "excuse me," and everything will be alright.

By the way. . .
When you see MT in this book, it stands for Medical Term.

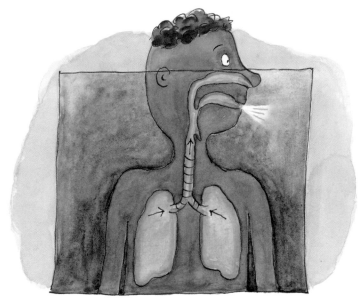

VOICE

One of the most obvious ways your body makes noise is through your voice. The actual noise, whether you're speaking or screaming or crying, is made by your vocal cords. Air from your lungs travels through your windpipe (MT: trachea) to your vocal cords, which makes them vibrate. It's similar to how a saxophone or clarinet works when you blow into it.

Your nose helps you make certain sounds, too. Try to read the next sentence while pinching your nostrils shut with two fingers: *Mike and Doug like milk and donuts.* See what we mean? And let's not forget your tongue. Try to read this next sentence without moving your tongue: *The thistle is sharp.* You may also have trouble with that sentence if you're missing your two front teeth!

Even when you whisper, you're still using your vocal cords. They're just moving in a different way. So, if your voice is hoarse and the doctor tells you to rest it, he means less talking *and* whispering. (Maybe write down what you want to say instead.)

Like the rest of your body, your vocal cords continue to grow until *you* stop growing. The most noticeable change likely happens when you're a teenager: your voice starts to sound more like an adult's. This is usually more obvious in boys because their voices get deeper. How deep depends on how big and how long their vocal cords grow. Similarly, the short, skinny strings of a violin make a high-pitched sound, but the long, thick strings of a cello sound low and deep. The same goes for your vocal cords.

True or False?

It's possible to break a crystal glass with an extremely loud voice. (*True.* But it's not easy. A microphone would help, and so would a very dainty glass.)

Doctor says:

"If you have a hoarse voice, you may have laryngitis."

BURPS

Every time you eat or drink, you're consuming air. A burp is the sound your body makes when it releases that air. But just as a sandwich is made up of bread, meat, tomatoes, lettuce, and mustard, air is a mix of different gases, mainly nitrogen and oxygen. So when you burp, you're releasing nitrogen and oxygen back into the air. Bubbly drinks contain mainly carbon dioxide gas, so when you drink them, your burp has carbon dioxide in it.

As you may have noticed, not all burps are the same. They can be big or little. The more that goes into your body, the more that comes out. A big gulp equals a big burp, and a little sip equals a little burp. Burps can be smelly or not, and the same rule applies: what goes in must come out!

A salami sandwich equals a salami-scented burp, and soda water equals a nobody-can-even-tell burp. And burps can be loud or quiet. The sound of a burp comes from the vibrations that the muscle (MT: upper esophageal sphincter) in the back of your throat makes when air passes by it. Think of a burp like a musical instrument. If you blow gently on a trumpet, it makes a soft noise; but if you blow hard, using a lot of air, it will be pretty loud.

#1 As of 2008, the world's loudest burp was made by Paul Hunn. His burp measured 107.1 decibels (Guinness World Records). To give you an idea of how loud that is, the sound of a chainsaw is between 95 and 115 decibels.

#2 Everyone burps to relieve pressure in their stomach. If you didn't burp, you'd probably look like you swallowed a beach ball and get a tummy ache!

True or False?

In some countries, it's a compliment to the cook to burp after a meal. (*True.* Just do a little country research before you start burping at the table. While some people appreciate it, others won't!)

HICCUPS

Hiccups start in the diaphragm, a pancake-shaped muscle that separates your chest from your tummy (MT: abdomen). When you hiccup, your diaphragm tightens, causing you to inhale quickly and automatically. Then your vocal cords close for a split second, which makes the *hic* sound.

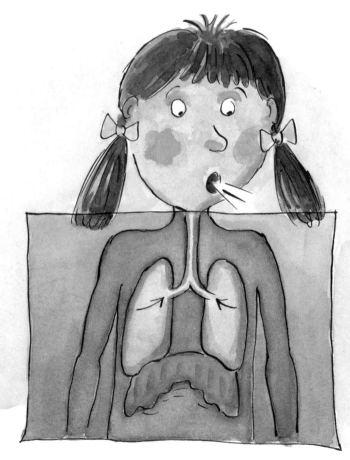

Two common things that cause hiccups are eating a big meal and drinking a bubbly drink. They both cause your stomach to expand and push on your diaphragm. Eating spicy food can also irritate the nerve that controls the diaphragm.

#1 The word *hiccup* actually sounds like what it is. Other examples of onomatopoeia are *buzz* and *splash*.

#2 Hiccups are still a bit of a mystery because doctors don't know their purpose.

True or False?

You actually start hiccupping before you are even born. (*True*. A pregnant mother can feel her baby's hiccups.)

True or False?

Drinking half a teaspoon of pickle juice every ten seconds a few times in a row will stop your hiccups. (*False*. This is one of several "silly" hiccup remedies that haven't been proven to work.)

STOMACH GROWLS

Everyone thinks that when your stomach makes rumbling noises (MT: borborygmi), it means that you are hungry. But it can rumble just as much when you are full. When you eat, the food goes from your mouth to your stomach, where it mixes with your digestive juices. As your food and digestive juices mix together, you swallow air, which can cause your stomach to growl.

From your stomach, the food enters your small intestine. Eventually, waves of muscle contractions (MT: peristalsis) move the waste out of your body.

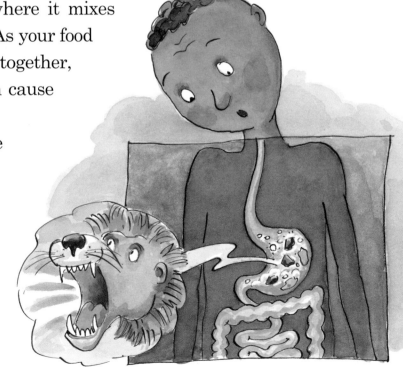

A couple of hours after your food is digested and your stomach is empty, your brain sends a message that it's time to eat again. Once the message is sent, even if you don't eat, the digestive juices start to flow and the stomach begins to churn. When you're hungry, the sound is more noticeable because there's no food to muffle or absorb it. The same effect can be heard with a dryer. If it's filled with two tennis balls and clothes, it's a lot quieter than a dryer with only tennis balls bouncing around in it.

To quiet down a noisy stomach, try eating several small meals throughout the day instead of a few large ones.

Doctor says:

"When I listen to your tummy with my stethoscope, I can hear stomach growls that you may not even know about."

FARTS

Just like burps, farts can be noisy or quiet, and they can be smelly or not. It may seem weird, but although they come from opposite ends of your body, burps and farts are a lot alike. Air becomes 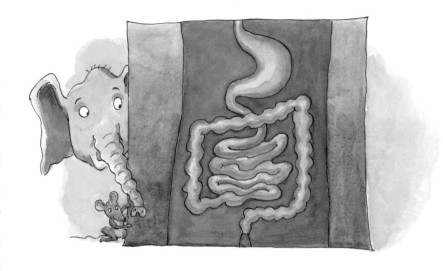 a fart as it moves down the digestive tract while the walls contract (remember peristalsis?). The sound of a fart comes from that air vibrating the muscle (MT: anal sphincter) at the end of your digestive tract, between your bum cheeks (MT: anus).

Sometimes farts are as quiet as a mouse or as loud as an elephant. How loud they are depends on how fast the air comes out of you and how tight the sphincter muscle is as the air leaves your body.

Once farts are released, you've probably noticed that they can be really stinky, and sometimes there's no smell at all. Like burps, their smell depends on the types of gases they contain. Some of the odorless gases come from the air you breathe in and swallow (nitrogen and oxygen), the bacteria that live in your intestines (hydrogen and methane), and bubbly drinks (carbon dioxide).

This mixture of gases gets stinky when you add hydrogen sulfide and molecules called mercaptans, which contain sulfur. As certain foods break down, they release sulfur into your body. The more of these foods you eat, the more sulfides and mercaptans your body produces (by bacteria in your digestive tract), creating smelly farts. Examples of sulfur-rich foods are cauliflower, eggs, and meat. Don't try to use this as an excuse not to eat them!

#1 Mercaptans are in the smelly spray that skunks let out when they are scared.

#2 Like carbon dioxide from smokestacks, methane is also a greenhouse gas. A large amount of methane comes from cows' burps and farts.

True or False?

Almost all animals fart. (*True.* If they have a tube-like digestive tract, they fart.)

True or False?

Elephants fart more than termites. (*False.* According to London's Science Museum's top ten list of farting animals, termites are in first place.)

Doctor says:

"Everyone farts to get rid of excess gas in the digestive tract."

SNEEZES

Loud or soft, many or few, sneezes come in all sorts of intensities and numbers. But they are all caused by the same thing – an irritation in your nose or throat. Irritants can be anything from allergens, such as pollen, to cold viruses. A sneeze

is just your body's way of trying to get rid of them – and fast! You never know when you're going to sneeze because it's *involuntary*, meaning your body does it without you actually thinking about it.

Have you ever noticed that some people sneeze whenever they see a bright light or step into the sun? This is called the photic sneeze reflex, and it's actually not that uncommon, occurring in 18 to 35% of the population. Confused nerve signals in the brain may be the reason this happens, but the truth is, no one has been able to determine the exact cause.

 **The speed of a sneeze (90 mph or 145 kph) is faster than the speed of a car on the highway.**

True or False?

Only humans are born with the ability to sneeze. (*False*. All animals sneeze.)

Doctor says:

"To stop the spread of germs, sneeze into your sleeve instead of into the air or your hands."

COUGHS

When you cough, your lungs force out air loudly and quickly. And that's about the only common thing when it comes to coughs.

Your coughs vary: they can be wet or dry, loud or soft, many or few. Coughing can be involuntary because your body usually does it without you even thinking about it, but you can also make yourself cough. Some coughs stick around for less than a minute, while others last much longer.

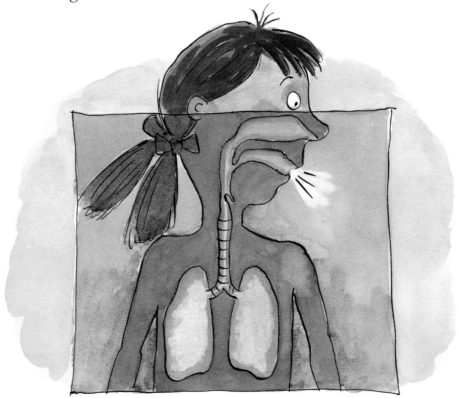

A cough is your body's way of getting rid of substances that irritate the passageway (MT: airway) that runs from your nose and mouth to your lungs. However, a cough can some-times be caused by something outside of your airway, like your heart, stomach, or even earwax.

The list of things that can cause you to cough is long, but common causes are infection – such as a cold (MT: viral upper respiratory tract infection) or flu – smoke, dust, and asthma. People with allergies to trees, grass, and pollen may cough in the springtime when everything is sprouting.

True or False?

Spinning around three times in a circle and then hopping on one foot is a good way to cure a cough. (*False*. But it does sound kind of fun!)

WHAT THE DOCTOR HEARS

The doctor uses a stethoscope to listen to some of the noises in your body. A stethoscope amplifies sound, much like when you put a glass to the wall to hear what's happening on the other side.

Three common areas that the doctor listens to are your heart, chest, and stomach. When the doctor listens to your heart, it usually sounds like this: *lub dub . . . lub dub . . . lub dub.* When the doctor listens to your chest, he probably asks you to take a big breath in and out to make the breathing sounds louder. They sound something like this: *whoosh . . . whoosh.* When the doctor listens to your stomach, he can hear growls that sound like this: *gurrrgle . . . gurrrgle.* So the next time you're at the doctor for a checkup, when he uses a stethoscope, now you know what he hears.

Doctor says:

"The *lub dub* sound of your heart is made by the closing of your heart valves. You have four valves, which close in pairs."

Doctor says:

"Heart murmurs are abnormal sounds that can be heard along with the *lub dub.* They may sound like a *whoosh* or a *swish.*"

Isn't it amazing what your noisy body can do!

Glossary

Bacteria, digestion, digestive juices, digestive tract, greenhouse gas, intestines, molecules, vagus nerve, vibrations, vocal cords.

Bacteria: Microscopic organisms that cause disease or infection.

Digestion: The process of breaking down food into nutrients the body can absorb.

Digestive juices: Substances produced by the body to aid digestion.

Digestive tract: A very long pathway that goes from your mouth to your anus, including your esophagus, stomach, and intestines.

Greenhouse gas: A gas in the earth's atmosphere that traps heat, such as carbon dioxide, methane, and nitrous oxide.

Intestines: The part of the digestive tract that runs from your stomach to your anus. Your small and large intestines work together to do important jobs, like absorb nutrients and water.

Molecules: The tiniest particles of a substance that retain all the properties of that substance.

Vagus nerve: Either of the tenth pair of cranial nerves that supplies sensory and motor fibers to the heart, lungs, and other organs in the main cavities of the body.

Vibrations: Rapid and rhythmical movements back and forth.

Vocal cords: Either of two pairs of membranes in the "voice box" that vibrate when air that is exhaled passes through them to produce sound.